MW01623296

Photo and set design by Wilson Chin

A scene from the Ars Nova production of *boom*.

boom

BY PETER SINN NACHTRIEB

DRAMATISTS
PLAY SERVICE
INC.

The world premiere of BOOM was presented by Ars Nova
(Jason Eagan, Artistic Director; Jon Steingart & Jenny Wiener, Executive Producers)

BOOM was originally developed at Brown/Trinity Playwrights Repertory
in the summer of 2007, directed by Kenneth Prestininzi.

For my science teachers

ACKNOWLEDGMENTS

Thanks to Kenneth Prestininzi for invaluable dramaturgy; Lowry Marshall for telling me to get rid of the third arm; Michelle Carter for being there at the birth of this play; Constance Crawford, Susannah Flood and Jimmy King for their innovation; Emily Shooltz, Jason Eagan, Alex Timbers, Megan Ferguson, Lucas Near-Verbrugghe, Susan Wands and everyone at Ars Nova for their generosity and making the show so awesome; Brown/Trinity Playwrights Rep and the entire summer 2007 crew; Howard Shalwitz, Elissa Goetschius, John Vreeke, Sarah Marshall, Aubrey Deeker, Kimberly Gilbert, Woolly Mammoth Theatre, Jerry Manning and Seattle Rep; Mark Orsini, Bruce Ostler and the Bret Adams Ltd. family; Lisa Steindler, Amy Mueller, Kent Nicholson, Tracy Ward, Will Dunne, Sean Daniels, Roy Conboy, Anne Galjour, Brian Thorstenson, Ken Clifton and the Smithsonian Tropical Research Institute, The Z Space Studio, The Playwrights Foundation, San Francisco State University, Harold and Ursula Nachtrieb, George Nachtrieb, Anne Zesiger, the entire Nachtrieb clan, and a special shout-out to more-than-a-boyfriend Mark Marino.

AUTHOR'S NOTE

On a year off from college, I landed a four-month job working for a marine biologist on a Caribbean island station (more like a spit of sand) just off the coast of Panama. For ninety days straight we woke before dawn, boated out two miles to a shallow reef, and observed fish spawn (specifically the Beaugregory Damselfish, *Stegastes leucostictus*, for those of you interested in the details). We recorded who was mating with whom, the number of eggs laid, the number of laid eggs cannibalized by the male, and many other exciting tidbits of fish data.

On occasional mornings, sudden, fierce, fast-moving storms would blow through as we worked in the water. First a strong wind, then hard rain that would transform the first couple feet of the sea to a froth. Down below, as the sky got dark, the fish would retreat into the crannies of the coral, as though they were readying for sleep/night. Meanwhile we hapless humans bobbed at the surface hoping that lightning wouldn't strike our boat. The storms would pass quickly, the sun would return, and the fish would gradually emerge into the open once again.

So, yeah: fish, sex, hiding from impending doom ... What a totally awesome play that would be, I thought to myself approximately ten years later. Am I right? Totally, right?

In college I majored in both theater and biology and I think this play might be an attempt to understand the relationship between the two. For me, both fields are attempting the same thing: to try and make some sense of the world in an epic and intimate way.

BOOM was originally developed at Brown/Trinity Playwrights Repertory (Lowry Marshall, Artistic Director), in Providence, Rhode Island, in the summer of 2007. It was directed by Kenneth Prestininzi and the production stage manager was Kristen Gibbs. The cast was as follows:

JULES .... Jimmy King
JO .... Susannah Flood
BARBARA .... Constance Crawford

BOOM received its world premiere by Ars Nova (Jason Eagan, Artistic Director; Jon Steingart and Jenny Wiener, Executive Producers), in New York City, on March 20, 2008. It was directed by Alex Timbers; the set design was by Wilson Chin; the costume design was by Emily Rebholz; the lighting design was by Marcus Doshi; the sound design was by Mark Huang; and the production stage manager was Alaina Taylor. The cast was as follows:

JULES .... Lucas Near-Verbrugghe
JO .... Megan Ferguson
BARBARA .... Susan Wands

BOOM was subsequently produced at Woolly Mammoth Theatre Company (Howard Shalwitz, Artistic Director), in Washington, D.C., in November 2008. It was directed by John Vreeke; the set design was by Thomas Kamm; the costume design was by Ivania Stack; the lighting design was by Colin K. Bills; the sound design was by Neil McFadden; and the production stage manager was William E. Cruttenden III. The cast was as follows:

JULES .... Aubrey Deeker
JO .... Kimberly Gilbert
BARBARA .... Sarah Marshall

CHARACTERS

JULES — a marine biology graduate student. Twenty-eightish, uncomfortable, excitable, literal.

JO — an undergraduate journalism student. Twenty-twoish, strong, skeptical, physical.

BARBARA — A natural history docent. Forties to fifties, buoyant, vulnerable, passionate, grand.

PLACE

Jules' subterranean university research lab that has been awkwardly fashioned into a living area. There are no windows. A large thick door is the only entrance. There is a fish tank, bubbling.

A sea of cabinets and drawers and other modes of storage dominate the walls.

This is also an exhibit.

There is a control station that looks like an old-style tech booth with giant levers, switches, analog knobs and such. And a timpani. Maybe some other special devices. This is Barbara's main area.

TIME

When we least expect it.

A NOTE ON BARBARA'S SPEAKING HABITS

Barbara occasionally uses a gesture instead of words. In the script I have placed the text that the gesture is intended to substitute in brackets. *[Like this!]*

The universe could so easily have remained lifeless and simple — just physics and chemistry, just the scattered dust of the cosmic explosion that gave birth to time and space. The fact that it did not — the fact that life evolved out of nearly nothing, some ten billion years after the universe evolved out of literally nothing — is a fact so staggering that I would be mad to attempt words to do it justice.

—Richard Dawkins, *The Ancestor's Tale*

There's something way down deep that's eternal about every human being.

—Thornton Wilder, *Our Town*

boom

Barbara bursts into the space.

She wears a nametag. She's just come from a meeting. Severe emotion is being wound up and contained.

A deep breath.

She puts something on the lab set that should have already been there. Fish food, maybe. She crosses to her area.

She pulls a big lever that, with a snap, shuts off the lights, except perhaps an interesting one around her.

Barbara picks up a set of timpani mallets and plays a brief, loud, introductory song that suggests danger. The ferocity of the playing contrasts her exterior calm. She's working something out hitting the drum.

Upon completion, she sets the mallets down, pulls another lever that turns on the lights of a fish tank.

Barbara pulls another lever that lights up the lab/apartment.

Jules, smiling, stares at Jo.

Jo, not smiling, stares at the fish tank.

JULES. Are you thirsty?
JO. No. *(Beat.)*
JULES. Can I take your coat?
JO. I'm not wearing a coat. *(Beat.)*

JULES. Can I take something from you and put it somewhere?
JO. Take off your shirt.
JULES. Pardon?
JO. You're not deaf.
JULES. Now?
JO. Did you want to fuck clothed?
JULES. You sure you don't want some water? Something stronger?
(Beat. Jules begins to unbutton his shirt. Jo stares at the fish.)
JO. What kind?
JULES. Um, Old Navy.
JO. The fish.
JULES. Oh. Beaugregory Damselfish.
Stegastes leucostictus. As they were called in ancient Greece.
That's Dorothy.
JO. Like the *Golden Girl*?
JULES. Like my younger sister. Her name, at least.
JO. Is she tall and mannish?
JULES. No, we're from Kansas.
You know … Dorothy?
My parents were into obviously relevant names.
JO. What'd they call you?
JULES. Jules.
After Jules Verne. I'm glad they didn't call me Vern, you know, because …
They had a hunch I liked aquatic things.
JO. Why?
JULES. I was a water birth. Unintentionally.
You never told me your name.
JO. Take off your pants. *(Beat. Jules slowly undoes his belt and pulls his pants down. He has difficulty disrobing. Balance issues? Forgetting to take his shoes off first? While doing this …)*
JULES. I only lived there till I was five. Kansas. Then we moved. My mom, two sisters and me did. My dad stayed. Sort of. I mean, I was five so I don't really know the actual details, you know, he, um, well, he stayed in Kansas. But left. In a way, I guess. More like sucked up. And then dropped. Into a field.

He wasn't really happy. Before. Hated being a weatherman. I think he hated Kansas. I remember that much. My five-year-old intuitive sense of … grief.

Anyway, we moved to Florida. Which, at least in my opinion,

was much nicer than Kansas. For a while. Until, well, until my sister decided to run outdoors in a hurricane right when a palm tree decided that it couldn't stay in the ground anymore, and my mom, other sister and I moved to Kenya. "Let's start fresh! Let's get away from it all!" my mom said. Although the "all" we were getting away from apparently didn't include malaria, and the fevers that malaria causes and the hallucinations that the fever causes and the hyenas that wait outside of medical tents ready to pounce on weak young flesh staggering out in a dream, and soon my mom and I moved here, where we've lived ever since. Except for my mom, who couldn't have picked a worse time to go on a tour of un-reinforced masonry in California. And here I am. *(Jules is now in his flannel boxer shorts, T-shirt, and socks.)* Where are you from? *(Jo kisses Jules actively, aggressively, maybe pressing him against a wall. Jules is frozen, stiff, not responding. Jo stops kissing, steps away. Beat.)*

JO. Massachusetts.

JULES. Oh. Nice.

JO. No, it's not.

JULES. Too many blizzards?

JO. I like snow. *(Beat.)*

JULES. Which part of Massachusetts?

JO. What was that?

JULES. Worcester?

JO. You said you loved to kiss.

JULES. When?

JO. "I love kissing, body contact, oral sex, and intensely significant coupling."

JULES. Oh right.

JO. You wrote that in your ad.

JULES. You remember things.

JO. That was the worst kiss ever.

JULES. It was surprising. I was surprised.

JO. That was a kiss of someone who does not enjoy the feel of lips.

JULES. I was hoping we could talk a little bit first. *(Jo smiles.)*

JO. I didn't come here to talk.

JULES. It would help me relax.

JO. Why?

JULES. I've never met anyone. This way.

JO. Which way?

JULES. With the help of technology.

JO. So?
JULES. I'm anxious.
JO. Why?
JULES. It's abrupt.
JO. And?
JULES. I've got some spanakopita. I just heated them up. So maybe we could — *(Jo goes to kiss Jules. He jumps back. Jo and Jules engage in a little cat-and-mouse. Maybe furniture is involved.)*
JO. Come here.
JULES. We should eat them while they're warm.
JO. This is not a game.
JULES. Warm and flakey.
JO. Sex! Now!
JULES. I appreciate your youthful eagerness, but you should understand that sometimes it takes me — *(Jo jumps on Jules, pushes him onto the ground or futon and gets on top of him.)* Holy crap.
JO. Stop thinking.
JULES. But —
JO. Start fucking.
JULES. I —
JO. Make me believe in life!
JULES. I can't just —
JO. Listen to your instincts!
JULES. I'm a homosexual. *(Jo stops. A beat.)* I think that's why I'm having a difficult time. *(Jo gets off of Jules.)* I should have mentioned it earlier.
JO. You didn't.
JULES. No.
JO. Why didn't you?
JULES. I thought it would make you not want to come over. Do you mind if I put my pants back on?
JO. You don't look gay.
JULES. Clothing-wise?
JO. You don't have gay eyes.
JULES. I'm wearing contacts right now so —
JO. Did you think I was a man?
JULES. What?
JO. Jo with an e?
JULES. Your name is Jo?
JO. The female spelling.

JULES. You sent me a picture.
JO. So you're bi-curious.
JULES. Oh, no. It's good to know your name.
JO. Did you just get born again? Are you a fundamentalist?
JULES. I'm a marine biologist.
JO. I don't get it.
JULES. Well, it's a field of science where we study —
JO. What is this?
JULES. I should put on some music.
JO. This is bullshit. *(Jules walks to an iPod with speakers.)*
JULES. I just bought one of those things that play all your songs.
JO. I don't have a lot of time! *(Barbara dums the timpani, lightly.)*
JULES. No. We don't.
JO. I'm twenty-two.
JULES. OK.
JO. It's Saturday night.
JULES. I think if I explained why —
JO. And there is an enormous world out there!
JULES. Uh-huh.
JO. Millions and millions of options.
JULES. It's a vibrant campus.
JO. And I only get to pick one at a time! Of all the recitals, ragers, and sex partners I could have selected from tonight, I picked this. I picked you. And … And …
JULES. Yay?
JO. And what if? What fucking if? *(Beat.)*
JULES. What if what?
JO. What if this is it?

What if I've set a series of events into motion that will doom me to be trapped forever in some desperate monotonous life and in my last breaths, when I look back at all the mistakes I've made, I'll remember this moment, now, as the moment I truly fucked it all up. And then I die.
JULES. Mm. *(Jo collects her bag, about to leave.)*
JO. Did you think about that?
JULES. Maybe.
JO. Did you think about what that means?
JULES. Don't go!
JO. Maybe you should think about that 'cause WE'RE ALL GONNA DIE! *(Barbara pulls down a large lever/switch, which makes*

a loud noise. Jo instantly collapses to the floor as though she has just been unplugged.)

JULES. Are you OK? Jo? Hello? *(Jules shakes Jo gently. She doesn't move. Checks for breathing, pulse. None.)* Shoot! Shoot shoot shoot. *(Jules looks around as though maybe someone could help, does that "emergency situation" shuffle of indecision. Finally, he kneels beside her, pinches her nose and slowly moves in to do rescue breathing. Jules is almost over her lips when Barbara flips the switch up. Jo jerks awake.)*

JO. AHHHH! *(Jules falls back.)*

JULES. Oh my goodness. Oh my goodness.

JO. Motherfucker.

JULES. That was shocking. *(Jo sits up, looks at the surroundings suspiciously, searching for a cause.)* Are you all right?

JO. I hate that question.

JULES. You weren't breathing.

JO. What's your point?

JULES. You were yelling at me, about to leave, and then you collapsed and weren't breathing.

JO. How old is this building?

JULES. Uh, I don't know. Forty, fifty years?

JO. Is it safe?

JULES. It was designed to be a bomb shelter. I don't … Do you need to lie down?

JO. *(To herself.)* What now?

JULES. I should bring you some water. A pillow. Spanakopita.

JO. *(To herself.)* Why are you doing this now?

JULES. Has that happened before?

JO. What?

JULES. What just happened.

JO. What just happened?

JULES. I'm being confused.

JO. Do you have bourbon?

JULES. I might.

JO. I'd like some bourbon.

JULES. Are you sure that's a good —

JO. On the rocks.

JULES. That's one of the truths of biologists. We always have ice. To freeze the things we kill.

And for drinks. *(Jo pulls out a steno pad from a backpack and scribbles copious notes. Jules opens a cabinet filled to the brim with plastic red frat-party cups. Gets two. He opens a cabinet filled to the brim with bottles of bourbon. He gets a bottle. He opens a stuffed freezer, retrieves some ice and prepares the drink. Perhaps he presses play on the iPod. Before returning to Jo with drinks, Jules heads towards the door and locks the deadbolt, or perhaps some futuristic impressive electronic locking knob.)* So. You go to school?

Here?

What are you majoring in?

JO. Do we have to talk?

JULES. No. No. *(Beat.)*

JO. Journalism.

JULES. Oh neat! Journalism. That's really neat.

JO. Yeah, it's neat.

JULES. What got you into that?

JO. The hair. Newscaster hair.

JULES. *(Not hearing.)* Oh. That's great!

JO. Never seen in the real world. Difficult to reproduce. Huge. That's powerful.

JULES. Mmm-hmm.

JO. Newscaster hair keeps the public from going insane. A soothing visual balance to that cruel graphic icon in the corner of the screen, some artist's rendering of the worst things. The world may be unraveling at a disturbing pace but lo, the hair is not: noble, reliable, immobile … it's the helmet we all need so badly to help us tolerate another day.

I wanted hair like that. *(Jules returns with the drinks, and a plate of spanakopita.)*

JULES. That's so great to be a journalist. Guardians of the First Amendment. Protectors of democracy. Deep Throat. What?

JO. You weren't listening.

JULES. I was making the drinks.

JO. What was I saying?

JULES. The ice was loud.

JO. You just want to talk about you?

JULES. I'm listening now.

JO. So, your family's dead?

JULES. Pardon?

JO. You have an entire family of dead people? Tornadoes, hyenas, whatnot.

JULES. Oh. Yes.

JO. That must suck.
JULES. Not exactly how I would phrase the —
JO. That must've really messed you up.
JULES. Everything does something.
JO. You're haunted by ghosts.
JULES. More by the laws of physics.
JO. What are all the thoughts rattling in your mind when you're not listening to the answers to questions you ask? *(Barbara hits the timpani. Jules looks upwards. Jules hands Jo the drink.)*
JULES. Cheers.
JO. I don't think so.
JULES. You don't like cheering?
JO. This isn't a date.
JULES. It isn't?
JO. A "casual encounter" does not have a toasting portion.
JULES. I was starting to feel a bond.
JO. Why am I here?
JULES. That's something we all want to know, isn't it? Is there a "purpose" to our form and substance? Or are we simply the random result of billions of years of chemical reactions and accidents influenced by pressures from the environment? Do we really —
JO. That wasn't my question.
JULES. It's what you asked.
JO. Why did you invite me to your … what is this, a lab?
JULES. My grant doesn't cover housing.

A drink. Or two. Conversation. Dinner. Building trust. A connection. Dessert. Probably some more drinks. Deep breaths. Focus. Keeping the goal clear. And then …

JO. What?
JULES. You know.
JO. No I don't.
JULES. What I wrote. Intensely significant coupling. *(Beat.)*
JO. You're a fag.
JULES. You shouldn't make assumptions based on that.
JO. I'm assuming that you fuck men.
JULES. That doesn't mean I wouldn't be able to with a woman.
JO. Have you ever?
JULES. No.
JO. See?
JULES. I've never had sex. With anything.

JO. Interesting.

JULES. I mean, of course, with myself. I'm familiar with the general sensations.

JO. How do you even know you're a gay?

JULES. The non-randomness of the erections.

JO. And still you've never.

JULES. I don't know if it's been a choice.

JO. Yes it has.

JULES. I haven't found the opportunity.

JO. There are thousands of men out there with low standards.

JULES. I know. Was that meant to be insulting?

JO. You have chosen to only make sweet love to your hand. Just like you chose to go online, post a misleading ad and have me here for … why am I really here?

JULES. The future of humanity depends on it. *(Barbara dums the timpani.)*

JO. I have a final project for my magazine class: "Find a story in an unconventional place that uplifts you. Personally. Deeply. Truly."

JULES. Are we changing subjects?

JO. "The following topics and items may not be used in your uplifting story: the sick, disabled, whales or any animal with fur, sports, war, poor people getting rich, rich people getting morals, underdogs in general, or anything that could be celebrated on a card."

JULES. I used to send those to myself from across town.

JO. "In other words: no tricks. No lies. Find a story that makes you feel honest, genuine, hope."

JULES. Neat.

JO. I'm having a hard time with it.

JULES. So … you went online to clear your head —

JO. This is the assignment.

JULES. Oh.

JO. Random sex as the last glimmer of hope in a decaying society. Everyone feels alone. Betrayed by their friends and families, their country, their dreams, their own selves. You know?

JULES. *(Doesn't know.)* Mmm.

JO. With nowhere to go in their normal depressing lives, people are forced to turn to the anonymous, the stranger. Alone, on laptops in isolated homes, a series of emails or an online chat brings two or more people together for a brief moment in time. No past. No future. All that matters is the moment.

They meet to fulfill each other's carnal needs, to find a moment of freedom, release, of sensory bliss that makes them forget how motherfucked up everything is. In no-strings sex, hope is still possible.

It's due Monday. *(Jo writes in her steno pad.)*

JULES. I could be uplifting.

JO. I should just make something up.

JULES. You can't do that.

JO. Why not?

JULES. You're a journalist. *(Beat.)*

JO. Where've you been the last few years?

JULES. On a desert island.

JO. 'Cause even *The New York Times* …

Really?

JULES. Well, more like a spit of sand …

JO. Really.

JULES. There was a volleyball net. That was nice. Of course there wasn't anyone else to —

JO. Sounds nice.

JULES. Very peaceful. Except when it rained. Corrugated tin.

JO. How long were you there?

JULES. Four years. Off and on. Nine months straight the last stretch. Lots and lots of data. Did you see *The Shining*?

JO. Yes.

JULES. It was much nicer solitude than that.

JO. Four years.

JULES. Yeah.

JO. Fish?

JULES. That's them.

JO. What about them?

JULES. Sleeping patterns. The significance of sunlight, radiation levels and extraterrestrial disturbances on diurnal fish activity, to be more specific. There are times of the year where storms come through in the morning, big fierce ones where the sky goes dark and it rains so hard that the first two feet of water is froth. It could be like ten A.M. and the fish will think it's time for bed. Time for bed, of course, is the wrong thing to say.

JO. Fascinating.

JULES. I've been researching this radical new sleeping pattern that's been taking place on this one reef I study. It's really really interesting.

JO. *(Finishing her drink.)* Mmm.

JULES. Like mind-warping, shockingly disturbing strangely interesting.
JO. I drank that fast.
JULES. Do you want to know what the strange new pattern is? *(Jo stares.)* They're going to sleep in the middle of the day! *(Jo stares.)* I know! I know.
JO. I'd like another drink.
JULES. Oh. Sure. Let me just … *(Jules doesn't move.)*
JO. My ice is lonely.
JULES. I feel like I've just started to share something very intimate.
JO. You have?
JULES. And I just can't stop.
JO. Could you first — *(Barbara flips a lever, lights change, maybe some underscoring music begins. Barbara maybe holds out charts or some visual aids.)*
JULES. It started in early July. I was at the reef, snorkeling and observing for the entire day, as I did every day, which explains my severe pruning condition … and there was this moment, 1:13, all of a sudden, the fish dart into the coral. Hiding. For a minute. Then they're back out. No perceivable change in light, no storm darkening the sky and frothing the water, maybe a barracuda but seriously …

Next day: 1:12, BAM! The fish hide. 1:14, swimmy swim swim. Every day it happens. And every day they hide for a minute or two longer. Full sunlight. No predators. And they're hiding. I have a great watch, by the way.
JO. You can just tell me where the bourbon is, and I can —
JULES. Last month, the fish came out in the morning, swam and ate for about twenty minutes, and then hid for the rest of the day. THE REST OF THE DAY. Sorry for shouting, but seriously. THEY'RE HIDING, SLEEPING, ALL DAY AND ALL NIGHT. And they're dying. Starving themselves in fear. Hundreds of corpses trapped in the coral. And no one is eating the carcasses, that precious defenseless energy.

There is something, out there, that is scaring the fish. To death. And it's scaring them more and more every day.

Because, perhaps, what they fear gets bigger and bigger. Or, maybe, closer and closer? *(Barbara dums the timpani, flips a lever and lights go back to normal.)*
JO. I thought you were going to share something personal.
JULES. You do realize what it could mean?
JO. You're going to have an awesome dissertation?

JULES. For life. The planet.

JO. Is it something about glaciers?

JULES. They know something.

JO. Who?

JULES. Fish may not be intelligent, Jo. But they are rational.

JO. I don't know any personally.

JULES. Well, you met Dorothy, so you know what she's about. Melanie, Alexis and JonJohn are a little more thoughtful.

JO. I don't see any others.

JULES. They're hiding. *(Jo writes in her steno pad.)*

JO. He hides on an island, or in the basement. Isolated. Obsessed about boring behavior in animals.

JULES. It terrifies me.

JO. This sad sexless hermit emerges online to lure another to his cave with the promise of pleasure only to be sabotaged by his soft lonely dick.

What is it that has triggered this man to take such a step on this particular night?

JULES. A comet. *(Barbara dums timpani.)*

JO. *(Not listening.)* What are those shocks in our lives that jolt us into action?

JULES. I think we're about to be hit by a comet. *(Barbara dums timpani.)* A really really big one. *(Barbara dums timpani a bit louder.)*

JO. Really.

JULES. There's something … a disturbance affecting the reef. Like a … a comet eclipse we can't sense. But they do.

JO. The fish?

JULES. I know it sounds —

JO. Stupid.

JULES. That's what they said at the conference.

JO. You've told people about this?

JULES. I tried to warn people. But they just coughed and mumbled me out of the Tampa Marriott. My professor told me I was an embarrassment to the department. He was trembling so hard that his Diet Coke sloshed out of the cup and wet his hand. I gave him a napkin, which resulted in one of the more complicated moments of awkwardness I have ever experienced. They would've asked me to leave at the end of the year.

That is, if they weren't about to be blown up in a giant comet explosion.

JO. Why haven't I read anything about this?

JULES. I know, isn't that creepy?
JO. Wouldn't an astronomer, maybe even a child with a telescope, have made an announcement?
JULES. I think they're being silenced.
JO. By whom?
JULES. The government.
JO. Ooooo.
JULES. They're trying to avoid pointless panic.
JO. When is this, this —
JULES. Globally catastrophic event?
JO. — Yeah, when's that happening exactly?
JULES. I don't know, precisely. *(Checks his watch.)* Seven minutes. Ish. If my calculations are correct.
JO. Of course you have calculations.
JULES. A quasi-triangulation that factors fish sleep time, comet speed, personal hunches … it's complicated. But accurate.

Don't be worried.

JO. I'm not worried.
JULES. Should I not have told you?
JO. I'm not worried.
JULES. Good. Because you're totally safe. In here. With me.
JO. Safe from what?
JULES. From my dark and evil personality that likes to trap women in my lab for experiments.

Just kidding! I meant you're safe from whatever might happen. Up there. I've spent the last week preparing. Sealing the room. Supplies. Extensive, extensive … you know.

I'm getting the feeling you don't believe me.

JO. I don't.
JULES. I'm such a bad convincer.
JO. I don't believe some meteor —
JULES. Comet.
JO. — Whatever —
JULES. — They're a lot bigger than meteors —
JO. — is going to strike Earth because fish have lost the will to live.
JULES. Maybe if I show you —
JO. I came here to get laid!
JULES. I'll show you the visual aids.
JO. And then write about how that made me feel good for a few minutes.

JULES. All the data's in the back.
JO. *(To herself.)* Please make this night worth surviving.
JULES. Don't go anywhere! *(Jules leaves. Jo finishes her glass, looks into the fish tank.)*
JO. Don't die, Dorothy. You have so much to live for! Tell your buddies to stop hiding and come on out. You have this beautiful, amazing tank. Enjoy your tank! *(Barbara dums the timpani, Jo grabs her head. She wobbles. To herself:)* WHAT? *(The bottle of bourbon empty, Jo walks back to the kitchen to look for more booze. The cabinet above is slightly ajar. She opens it. It's completely full of bourbon. She opens the adjacent cabinet. It is packed completely with health energy bars. With increasing speed, Jo begins to open every cabinet and drawer in the back wall area. They are packed with hundreds and hundreds of the same items: candles, matches, batteries, first aid, gas masks?, Tasty Bites Indian food, survivalist books, toilet paper. A cabinet full of seeds and plants. She opens one final cabinet full of tampons and diapers, which all fall out of the cabinet and onto Jo and the floor. She puts her glass down and heads for the door and tries to open it. The door is locked. She tries again. She struggles with it. She moves away from the door and sits. Jules enters with printouts, charts, and a map.)*
JULES. I keep this all in the bathroom. Literature always seems to migrate in that direction so I just keep it there.
There are tampons and diapers on the floor.
JO. They fell out.
JULES. Oh.
JO. I opened the cabinet.
JULES. I see. *(Beat.)*
JO. It was full of tampons and diapers.
JULES. Yes. That's the tampon-and-diaper cabinet.
JO. It's full.
JULES. I just went to Costco.
JO. Why?
JULES. I didn't realize that there were so many different sizes and shapes.
JO. This is fucked up.
JULES. Did you, oh, did you need one?
JO. I'm going to take off now.
JULES. Sure you don't want —
JO. I have an article to write.
JULES. I've got plenty.

JO. I DON'T WANT A FUCKING TAMPON! *(Jo walks to the door. She looks at the knob, not touching it.)* WHAT THE FUCK?
JULES. Are you all right?
JO. I CAN'T LEAVE!
JULES. Why not?
JO. I am unable to open the door. *(Beat.)*
JULES. I locked it.
JO. Let me out.
JULES. Just let me show you my calculations — *(Jo runs to the fish tank.)*
JO. I will knock this over.
JULES. There are fish in there.
JO. Open the door and the fish live.
JULES. I can't. I can't I can't. *(Jo pushes the tank a bit off the edge. Jules reveals a map of the world. There's a target marked on it with concentric circles expanding outwards.)* There's an archipelago of islands. Near Panama and Colombia. That's where it's heading at a thousand kilometers a second. Striking any minute. I think. You would not want to be there right now. Or anywhere above ground really.
JO. Why?
JULES. I don't think comets have reasons why they —
JO. WHY DID YOU LOCK THE DOOR?
JULES. I don't want you to die! *(Barbara hits the timpani. Jo wobbles.)* Are you all — *(With a yell, Jo karate-chops Jules. He falls to the ground, and Jo grabs the keys from Jules' pocket. Barbara starts playing the timpani. A low rumble that will grow.)*
JO. AHHHH!
JULES. Ow. Ow.
JO. Fucking crazy gay virgin motherfucker. *(Jo runs for the door. Rumbling gets louder and louder.)*
JULES. Wait! WAIT!
JO. Campus police is going to kick your ass!
JULES. Don't you hear the deafening noise?
JO. Whatever!
JULES. Noooooooo — *(The sound gets very loud. Blinding white light shoots through the cracks of the door. Jo looks like she's getting an electrical charge shooting through her when she touches it. A comet hits the planet Earth and is somehow simulated. Barbara shuts off the main show lever. Sound and lights out or alter. Jo and Jules are frozen.)*

BARBARA. And we're going to hold for a moment there. *(Barbara walks onto the stage, smiling. Over the course of the monologue, she perhaps empties more cabinets of their contents, turns over furniture so that perhaps all that remains upright is the fish tank. Maybe she upturns the rock or aquatic feature in the tank too.)* I wanted you to know that the actual noise was louder. And there was a lot of shaking of things. Some flames. Dust. Miscellany falling from elevated places. Chaos. Terror. *(A gesture of chaos and terror, maybe toppling a few things.)* We have tried our best to reproduce that, here. Alas, there's only so much we can do. What with the limitations: physical, cognitive, budgetary. I just wanted to underscore the … girth of the moment. Big Girth. *(A gesture of large girth.)*

This is, in fact, that well-known moment in time. What we now refer to as "The Boom"? Everyone is familiar with that term? I will assume your silence or words mean "yes."

We're all familiar with the general circumstances of the event? That he was correct? The "fish" were correct? The impact did indeed *[occur]*?

And most everything, almost all forms of life on the planet, you know, just … *[ceased to live]*.

Pretty unfortunate, really. That there are moments in time where everything has to go like that. Dolphins especially. But, alas, it is a brutal history that we are all a part of. *(With increasing passion.)* A history that goes back millions and millions and millions of years. Back to that fresh rock, angry water, that sludgy mix of young amino acids sloshing about in the soup with reckless handsome abandon until CRACK! The perfect bolt of energy in the perfect spot and there you have it: the world's first protein!

Motherfucker!

So begins this amazing story of change, of innovation, of great catastrophe, of LIFE. MY GOD, WHAT A STORY OF LIFE IT IS!

I'm Barbara. *(A gesture towards her tag.)* Just in case you *[forget]*.

I'm … I'm really not supposed to be talking at all.

But sometimes what we're supposed to do — *[isn't what we should do]*.

Right? Right? Right.

"The Boom." It's not just about a loud noise. It's the event: a sudden, radical change in the state of things. *(Barbara has walked back to her station. She flips a lever and the stage goes dark. Sounds of destruction above? The fish tank remains lit and bubbling. A moment of silence. Jules groans, perhaps sounding like he's emerging from under a pile of rubble.)*

JULES. Oh my goodness …

I was … I was right! HA! I was … *(Jules rushes to the tank and looks in.)* Hello there. Hello hello hello. One two three four, you're all there.

I can't believe it. I mean, I can. My data. My sweet, hunky, accurate data. But then I was surrounded by all that naysaying and negativity.

Scientists are such doubters. "Show me proof," "Did you think of this? Did you factor this?" I mean, sure you gotta question but, come on, stop being jealous and take a leap once in a while!

But guess who's right now, Professor Vandikamp? Who's your favorite co-author now? Have another Diet Coke 'cause hello, Vindication!

Bittersweet, of course. I mean this is pretty severe. And terrible. Devastating. Mmm … We should have a ceremony, you know, light a candle. Remember the favorite things that are gone. Ice cream. What do you miss, Jo?

Jo? Jo, are you…? *(Jules pulls out a flashlight. Turns it on, shines it around. He finds Jo lying unconscious on the floor.)* Shoot! Shoot shoot shoot. *(He feels her pulse. He shakes her gently. She doesn't move. He assesses her.)* Why did you have to be so close to the door?

Come on. *(Slaps her/shakes her.)* Wake up. We've got to fulfill our destiny! *(Barbara pulls lever, Jo pops awake.)*

JO. AAAAAAAAAAAAAAAAAAAAAAAAAAAAAAAAAAAAA-AAAAAAAAAAAAAAAAAAAH!

JULES. Oh! Oh thank goodness!

JO. MOTHERFUCKER!

JULES. Yes, yes, wake it up! Wake yourself up, Jo, 'cuz we're alive! We are safe and breathing and alive!

JO. Where am I?

JULES. It's OK, Jo! We're OK! We were deep enough. The duct tape seems to be working!

I think you had one of those things again.

JO. It's dark.

JULES. I know, I didn't see it as clearly, but I think you were out for a —

JO. I can't see!

JULES. That's because we're plunged into blackness 'cause everything above ground has …

JO. What?

JULES. I have lanterns and candles. Let me put out some items that emit, and maybe things won't seem so — You had no pulse. *(Jules begins to put out lanterns, LEDs, candles, things that emit.)*

JO. The motherfuck is this.

JULES. No breaths and no pulse.

JO. What just happened?

JULES. I should have stored a crash cart.

JO. Everything above ground has what?

JULES. All I know is that it was large. The … comet was large. Approximately the same size as the one that hit at the Permo/Triassic, before the dinosaurs, and that one, well, wow … Ninety-five percent of all species, all species on the planet just …

JO. Right.

JULES. Don't panic. That still leaves …

JO. Five?

JULES. Animals, plants, fungus, bacteria … protected, lucky somehow.

And there's got be a special government human cave. Governments have caves for events like these. As do militias. And perverts. *(Jules moves toward Jo.)* It would be silly if we were the only ones to — *(Jo grabs a bottle of bourbon and holds it out as defense.)*

JO. Stay the fuck somewhere else! *(Barbara flips a lever and the lights change.)*

BARBARA. He was right about the bacteria. And the fungus. Quite a number of arthropods survived as they are wont to do. Little bastards.

He was also sort of right about the "special government cave." There was a large one buried deep in a mountain populated with, one can assume, a collection of individuals deemed most valuable by the society: thinkers, athletes, donors.

Alas, despite the clever civic planning, a sudden mudflow rushed into the artificially built cavern causing a catastrophic collapse of the structure … accelerated by what would appear to be severely flawed government construction.

On the bright side, the calamity managed to preserve parts both hard and soft and become one of the most astounding fossil deposits of the period, what is now known as the "Halliburton Shale."

(Barbara flips a lever, lights change. Jo has the bottle pointed at Jules. She pulls out her cell phone and dials.)

JO. Do you do this every Saturday?

JULES. What?

JO. Some people dress up as a coach and lick feet. But for you, it's this.

JULES. This is a catastrophic event.

JO. Bullshit!

JULES. Denial. Anger.

JO. Come on.

JULES. What you're feeling is very common.

JO. Why is the tank still working?

JULES. It's attached to a car battery.

JO. How convenient.

JULES. I have lots of things attached to batteries. Hand cranks for later. We'll take shifts.

JO. Goddamn Verizon!

JULES. It's not working, is it?

JO. If a huge "comet" really hit —

JULES. — which it did —

JO. And that was really causing a … a —

JULES. A violent storm of choking dust causing freezing endless night.

JO. If that was really happening, we'd be dead.

JULES. But we're not!

JO. You're not smart or practical enough to have sufficiently prepared for the end of the world.

JULES. I wish I knew how to convince you.

JO. I wish I'd been a cheerleader instead of smart and different! I'd be perky. I'd have tons of BFFs to share my deepest feelings with. I'd have a boyfriend. We'd have gone on a nice date tonight. We would have had hot heterosexual sex.

I wish I was normal, had normal experiences and maybe just a moment where something mildly pleasurable happens … but instead, I meet a faggy psycho like you into some Cormac McCarthy *Road Warrior*-meets-*Survivor* fantasy apocalypse whateverthefuckthisis bullshit where you want to pretend that you're lucky when nobody else is.

You're not a lucky person! And neither am I.

We're the kind of people who get the assignment wrong, who get stuck with the basement lab, whose bodies are cursed and sabotage their intentions.

We're not the people who should survive. *(On Jo's last word she has grabbed the doorknob.)* So go fuck yourself and your fish and your fantasy and see — *(Barbara flips a lever and Jo collapses. Jules runs to Jo, stands over her. Barbara flips the lever back up.)* Ya later! Shit.

Shit shit shit.

JULES. You just —

JO. I know.

JULES. The third time.

JO. I collapse a lot! *(Beat.)* I can't open the door.

JULES. You must be getting bruisey.

JO. *(To herself.)* You won't let me open the fucking door.

JULES. There's got to be some reason.

JO. *(To herself.)* This is actually happening?

JULES. It is.

JO. *(To Jules.)* Everything above ground?

JULES. Everything.

JO. Motherfucker. *(Jo cries. Jules sits next to Jo, turns. In a very unsuccessful way, Jules stiffly pats Jo on the shoulder or attempts a terrible hug. Jo moves away.)*

JULES. I have a large crate of books on grief and loss.

JO. No, thanks.

JULES. I figured there would be emotions. It's totally natural.

JO. I don't need a book.

JULES. I find them very soothing.

JO. You don't know me.

JULES. We have some time. *(Beat.)* You know, it's like your body's reacting to something. There's some trigger that —

JO. How much time?

JULES. Until the dust settles. Barely a blip. On a geological scale.

JO. Define blip.

JULES. Two years. Ish. Twoish. When, you know, the sun's energy is once again able to penetrate the atmosphere. I could be wrong.

JO. How wrong?

JULES. It could be two to four years. *(Jo runs to the door. Barbara pulls lever, Jo collapses. Barbara pulls another lever, lights change and Jo and Jules freeze.)*

BARBARA. I know you are probably asking the same question in your minds as many many other groups have done before you. One of the great unknown mysteries of this story: What are the "fish" doing at this time?

We know they are alive, of course. That the water remained sufficiently oxygenated, the food supply remained steady. But how were they? Distraught? Confused? Relieved? Were they observing what was taking place on the other side of the glass or was this a time for introspection? Deep fish thinking.

We don't know. It's a big *[mystery]* …

Take a moment now to imagine for yourselves: What would it be like. To be in that room, right then, the most important moment in history.

Would you want to be fully aware of the perilous situation that surrounds you and what was at stake? Or would you prefer to be blissfully ignorant of your role in the fate of the world?

What if that perilous moment was today? *(Barbara pulls lever, lights return to normal. Jules carries Jo to the futon.)*

JULES. Two to four awesome years. We can get to know each other better. Have some amazing talks. Share our darkest fears and secrets. Write. Paint. Actually finish a Thomas Pynchon novel. Mate. *(Barbara pulls lever, Jo wakes up.)*

JO. Mother-fffffff.

JULES. Is it something about doors? Do you have a problem with doors?

JO. Can you kill me?

JULES. Pardon?

JO. You must have some cyanide, just in case. Force it down my throat.

JULES. I do not! *(Jo finds a plastic bag, hands it to Jules.)*

JO. Here.

JULES. What?

JO. Pull it over my head. Hold it around my neck and don't let go for an hour.

JULES. Ew!

JO. It'll be a lot easier if you kill me.

JULES. Why?

JO. I don't want to be alive for this! *(Beat.)*

JULES. I think we should eat something …

JO. This is so unfair.

JULES. — I bought some wild salmon at the farmer's market —

JO. This is hell. A French hell.

JULES. Don't you see how significant this is?

JO. Kill me!

JULES. We have to rebuild the human race! *(Barbara hits a gong, or that Chinese cymbal that goes up in pitch at the end, or plays some wooden blocks faster and faster, or she chants so she sounds like one of those dramatic wailing women that seem to dominate soundtracks of Ridley Scott movies.)*
JO. So that's what this is about.
JULES. We are a sprig.
JO. A what?
JULES. A sprig. The beginning of a new branch. On the great bush.
JO. What bush?
JULES. The bush of life! *(Barbara does whatever it is she did before, a little shorter this time.)*
JO. Motherfucker.
JULES. Many key moments in the evolution of a species are when there are funnels. Bottlenecks. Catastrophes and opportunities and where a lucky few squeeze through. A couple frogs get stuck on a raft of twigs, sail across the ocean and leap onto a new chunk of land where they become the ancestors of every frog species in the New World. When the dinosaurs disappear, shrews hiding in the rocks begin to take over the newly vacant niches and voilà, look at all the mammals! And later, one or two fashion-forward apes decide to drop out of the trees and walk on their hind legs. And they think they're so cool, they only mate with each other, leaving the tree apes behind and eventually, maybe, becoming you and me. *(Beat.)*
JO. So?
JULES. We're a funnel!
JO. You said we're a sprig.
JULES. Same thing.
JO. A funnel and a sprig?
JULES. I changed imagery.
JO. You shouldn't do that.
JULES. I didn't intend to —
JO. You suck at communicating.
JULES. Well, it's an extraordinary, exciting, huge responsibility to be where we are. And we have to … do what we have to do.
JO. Document and report the last moments of the human species?
JULES. We are going to use those diapers. We're going to use those diapers and grow that bush.
JO. "Intensely Significant Coupling."

JULES. It's going to be really difficult.
JO. To fuck?
JULES. We've got to. No matter how terrible it will be. *(Barbara pulls a lever, lights change.)*
BARBARA. There are a lot of words being used here. Words that may be unfamiliar: "Funnel," "Sprig," "Motherfucker." These words and many others have no direct synonyms in our modern tongue.

I have prepared a pamphlet with many helpful and fascinating definitions. If you wish to investigate further. Which people do every day. Some people think this is the best part of the whole museum.

I wish they would sell it before you attend. It would help with your understanding of the story, with grasping the sheer magnitude of *[what is going on]* but clearly, I'm not the one in charge here. I'm not the one who makes those decisions. I am but a pellet in a jar being throttled by a thoughtless *[hand]*.

It's in the gift shop. They're on sale. *(Barbara pulls a lever, lights back.)*
JO. I hate babies.
JULES. No one hates babies.
JO. They bother me physically, philosophically and symbolically.
JULES. You don't really mean that.
JO. I dropped a spoonful of yogurt on a baby once just to see what would happen.
JULES. Why?
JO. I hate babies. I hated being a baby. And I'm not a mother.
JULES. Not yet.
JO. You don't want eggs from this basket. They're cracked. And did you happen to notice that there are frequent moments when I don't circulate blood? I am not meant to be a creator and caretaker of spawn.
JULES. I think a lot of women feel that way until they have one of their own.
JO. Which women?
JULES. I was speaking more generally.
JO. How many am I supposed to have?
JULES. As many as we can.
JO. And if I have daughters, do you have to fuck them too?
JULES. No! No.

I would inseminate them, but not —
JO. Ew!
JULES. It's not going to be easy.
JO. I'm not a factory. I'm not your experiment.

JULES. This is not some test in a lab! I mean, we're being tested and we're in a lab but this is … for maybe the first time in our lives, we could really make an impact.

Ancestors to the new line of human species. You and me. Don't you think that's a teeny bit awesome?

JO. What has the human species ever done for you?

JULES. What?

JO. Maybe a big ball hitting Earth was perhaps a suggestion from something that maybe it was time to change the shit up.

JULES. Comets don't have intent.

JO. Maybe it's time to end our reign of terror and die and decay and become soil. Our bodies will compress under peat and form wells of oil for some future, entrepreneurial beetle to drill for and burn.

JULES. Aren't you a little young to be cynical?

JO. Look at all the acts humans commit across the planet with casual, unconscious cruelty.

We deserve to be blown up.

JULES. Gobbledy!

JO. What?

JULES. Who, exactly, is this judge who thinks we deserve to be blown up? "The great sender of the objects"?

JO. The universe.

JULES. You shouldn't characterize the forces of the universe as a person.

JO. Why?

JULES. It's silly.

JO. Billions of people disagree.

JULES. You really think there's some *Wizard of Oz*-type person, judging us, pulling levers and altering our fates? *(Barbara sneezes.)*

JO. Sometimes.

BARBARA. *(Not too loudly.)* Excuse me.

JULES. Maybe it's too soon to be having discussions.

JO. You shouldn't have picked me for this.

JULES. You picked it.

JO. How?

JULES. You're the only one who answered the ad.

JO. "Have sex to change the course of the world."

JULES. It could.

JO. I thought that meant you were good at it!

JULES. We're going to survive.

JO. No we're not.
JULES. We're going to survive and we're —
JO. I am not having a fucking baby!
JULES. OK. OK. We'll see about that.
JO. Is that a threat?
JULES. I'll just get the salmon. *(Jo gets up, finds her steno pad and begins to write furiously. Jules exits to the storage room.)*
BARBARA. *(Whispering.)* Isn't this fascinating? The drama of survival. Such vigorous ideas and opinions and passions. I bet none of you knew the gritty details of what transpired during this story.

We are fortunate to know so much about our origins … You'd think that the importance of sharing this knowledge would be apparent to everyone … that it has so much impact on you and me, on who we are …

Here comes a juicy part.
JO. *(To herself.)* What do you want from me? Do you have some purpose for my existence or are you just being cruel? *(She looks at the fish.)* I hope you feel guilty. Swimming and hiding like happy little assholes.

You should have warned smarter, fitter, more attractive people. Of the billions of human bodies that could be breathing next to you, you end up with the mutant and the fag.

I could eat you if I wanted. I hope you know that. Your fate is out of your control. *(Jules enters, a little shaken. Jo writes.)*
JULES. I don't think you'll have to turn in your paper.
JO. I write everything down that's happened.
JULES. I should do that too.
JO. I need to write it down.
JULES. I should write more checklists.
JO. I will find a way to get out of here no matter what you or my body does.
JULES. No need to panic.
JO. I'll make you want to push me out.
JULES. The storage room caved in.
JO. What storage room?
JULES. The one in the back with the majority of life-sustaining supplies. The fridges are crushed. Protective space-age wrappers have been torn. There's water leaking in …
JO. So?
JULES. Most of the food was in there.

JO. The salmon is ruined?
JULES. I'm not sure if we have enough. To survive. *(Barbara pulls a lever. Lights change.)*
BARBARA. Ohhhhh. Oh oh oh. There is trouble!

The food is gone, the air is thin, the fan has really been hit! What oh what are they going to do? And it's gotta be something *[huge]*! *(Beat.)* I would really like to tell you how I was conceived. *(She looks to see if the coast is clear, takes the stage.)* It was a hot sticky sticky hot day. The type of day where you are hoping for someone to breathe on your face for a bit of wind. The type of day when your outstretched hand disappears in a haze of vapor. The type of day when clothing becomes more of a nuisance than a much-appreciated social construct.

My mother-to-be was by the shore, sprawled under a tree whose shade offered nothing. The water looked refreshing but the violent surf, fear of the unseen, and a mild allergy to salt kept her from moving too close. She lay back on the hot sand, opening her body wide so that any movement of air would have maximum contact.

My father-to-be was in the sea, a short ways away, theoretically hunting for food but really floating on his back and daydreaming.

Oddly comfortable with his body image, he had stripped himself of all his clothes, save for a wristwatch he wore for sentimental reasons. His dreams were vivid. Having recently pledged to not actively pleasure himself in an effort to bring more focus and productivity to his life, his dreams skewed towards filling the void that his hands had left.

He dreamt his naked body was swimming in a pool filled with cool, vibrating, lubricated marbles that gently rolled and rubbed and activated his exterior, asking it to be alert. Reaching out through the moistness he touched skin reaching out towards his. It was the skin of my mother.

Not her actual skin, of course, which was … *[on the shore]*.

It was what he had envisioned for years to coat her flesh. Warm and wet, colorful and perfect. The imaginary touching grew, back and forth motions intensified, a feeling so beautiful and overwhelming surged until my father-to-be, in his dream, and in the water, exploded.

My mother-to-be heard a slight popping noise above the surf, glanced outwards but could only see a discoloration of the haze as she felt particles land on her skin that were refreshingly cool.

What she did not see was the fertile fluid that had erupted out of my father-to-be one hundredth of a second before he himself erupted, pushed by the energy of the blast quickly and invisibly towards the shore where the smallest of portions had just the right angle to land inside my mother-to-be, swim with passion and feist into her core, fertilize an egg, and make me.

It took a number of years to figure out how that all happened, and it's been a party story ever since. I've embellished of course, as we are wont to do, but I remain faithful to the story's intent. I am passionate about my stories. *(She looks up.)* PASSIONATE!

I'm sorry. I'm really really not supposed to be … *[talking]*.

I just thought … since we … I could share how this is *[personal]* …

The theme, the resilience of life, against all odds blah blah blah and such …

It's just … this is the last time I get to do this. *(Barbara flips a lever and the "lab" lights up. The fish tank bubbles. Time has passed. The space feels lived in and depleted. Lighting has been set up in a manner that appears more thought out than before. Nests made out of rubble. Pillows and blankets are set up by the door. Cabinets are empty. Trash piled up: foil wrappers, cans, etc. … There are stacks of notepads. Maybe forty or fifty of varying styles, Jo having searched for whatever was available to write on. We hear noises of Jules manically searching through rubble somewhere in the back. Jo is writing. Her hair is wild. There are bruises on her head, arms, if we can see them. Jo has Jules' watch on her wrist.)*

JO. *(Writing.)* Escape attempt number three thousand two hundred and four: *(She puts her pad down, begins to stretch and prep for a run. She catches Dorothy looking at her.)* Don't. I know what you're gonna … I know, D, I know. I anticipate failure. But you never know, it just needs to be different once.

Yeah, well, so are you. You always chew on the same fake plant, how desperate is that. Sorry. You mean well. You're understanding, a wonderful listener. I'm sorry for the things I say. Sometimes I say things.

I promise this will be the last time. *(Barbara hits the timpani.)*

JULES. Oh!

JO. If I fail, if you see me again …

JULES. *(Vaguely orgasmic.)* Oh God.

JO. *(To the fish.)* If I put my arm in your tank, please eat it.

JULES. Yes! Yes!

JO. Start at the knuckles. They're tender. Please. Eat me up.
JULES. Wow! Wow! Wowie.
JO. Excuse me. *(Jo hides behind something and gets in an attack pose. Jules pops in from the storage room, panting. Jules enters with a paper bag in his hand. He's limping, a makeshift brace around one of his legs.)*
JULES. Two minutes ago I was about to give up hope. I was about to eat concrete just to feel like there was food in my stomach. But then … Pow! Surprise! It's almost a miracle but I don't believe in those. *(Moving into Jo's space.)* Oh, Jo Jo Jo, you are not going to *believe what I've just — (Jo yells, karate-chops Jules on his bad leg.)* OW!
JO. You think I'm not listening?
JULES. OW!
JO. I'm always listening, motherfucker.
JULES. Right in the tenderness.
JO. You were warned!
JULES. You didn't have to do that!
JO. I'll do it again.
JULES. I was coming to share —
JO. Stay out of my room!
JULES. Don't you want to know what's in the bag?
JO. I don't.
JULES. It's an amazing surprise!
JO. I don't like your surprises!
JULES. I promise you there's nothing —
JO. You've promised before.
JULES. It's not the —
JO. Your words mean nothing.
JULES. It's not the —
JO. Words words words.
JULES. It is not the baster! *(Beat.)*
JO. It kind of looks like a baster.
JULES. You melted the baster. Remember the fumes?
JO. I don't know if there's another baster.
JULES. There was only one baster.
JO. You just want me to believe there's only one baster.
JULES. Sheesh. I try something a little desperate once and you dangle it over my head —
JO. Nineteen times.
JULES. That is an exaggeration.

JO. Five times with a baster while I was sleeping, three with a syringe, twice with your finger, once with the paper towel tube like a blow gun, once with a booby-trapped toilet, once trying to get me to take a "bubble bath," once crying hysterically about feeling like an orphan and begging, three times getting me drunk and trying to get me to wear a Jake Gyllenhaal mask, and twice masturbating onto a tampon.

As if that would be good timing.

JULES. I don't know what to say right now.

JO. Read it again.

JULES. Do I —

JO. Read it! *(Jules pulls out a crumpled piece of paper from his pocket.)*

JULES. "I, Jules, know that it's not right to try and fertilize my post-apocalyptic cohabitant against her will."

Even if that's the only hope for humankind and —

JO. Keep going.

JULES. "And I will not attempt to inseminate Jo against her will again."

Though you should really come to your senses and see what an amazing —

JO. And?

JULES. "And I know that if I attempt to inseminate Jo, she has full permission to break my leg." *(Jo releases Jules.)* I think it's infected.

BARBARA. Oh no.

JO. Gotta go.

BARBARA. I forgot … *(Jo checks the watch, begins deep breaths, warms up. Barbara racks her brain.)*

JULES. It's about food, by the way.

JO. Clear the thoughts.

JULES. I figured out a way to get more food!

JO. Ignore the triggers.

JULES. We will not starve today.

JO. Focus on the task.

JULES. A little bit of good news …

JO. Vanquish the doom.

JULES. Could've been a nice moment.

BARBARA. *(Quietly.)* Oh nuts.

JO. *(Psyching herself up.)* Yes! This is a nice moment.

JULES. You … really?

JO. A non-threatening positive moment.

JULES. Your smile makes me tense.
JO. *(Beginning a slow ramp up towards heading to the door which should end in a full run.)* Good good Happiness Sunlight Joy Bicycles Flamenco Dancing Warmth Fun Time Gentle Wind Please Please Please PLEASE — *(Barbara pulls a lever, Jo and Jules freeze.)*
BARBARA. TIME HAS PASSED.

I usually mention that before this portion but as you can tell *[I'm a little distracted]*.

If you wish to know what transpired during the intervening months, I have prepared an exhaustive transcript of all omitted events which can be found in my really amazing pamphlet at the shop. It's both fascinating and devastating what happened over time. A gradual, steady erosion … Much like my belief in good.

I'm kidding, of course, not really sort of. I'm kidding. I mean, my belief in good didn't erode.

It was more like a hard rock in the face that will never heal and I'm totally kidding. I love good. I love management. I love the management of this exhibit and their eternal wisdom and incredible rock-aim. They know exactly how to hit you where it bleeds, deep and I should not be talking about workplace politics.

I should not have mentioned that today is the last day. I should not be discussing something that obliterates my entire *[purpose of living]*.

Time. Has. Passed. *(Barbara pulls the lever. Jo runs full steam at the door and handle hard, hoping some momentum might help push the door open, Barbara pulls her lever and she promptly collapses onto the blankets and pillows. Barbara quickly turns lever up, Jo regains consciousness.)*
JO. Motherfucker.
BARBARA. *(Muttering.)* Motherfucker. *(Beat, not really listening to each other.)*
JULES. I won't ask if you're OK.
JO. Three thousand two hundred and four: failure.
JULES. I'm concerned for your well-being, but I know not to verbalize that.
JO. That was the last attempt.
JULES. I know I'm not supposed to share my thoughtful scientific theories about why you fall and cuss so much.
JO. *(To fish.)* Help me, D.
JULES. Won't even let me check your blood pressure.
JO. You are my only hope. *(Jo drops her arm into the fish tank. A beat and then with an increasing rhythm.)*

JULES. Are you warm?
JO. Do you ever give up?
JULES. Why should I give up?
JO. Two hundred and sixty-seven days.
JULES. I know.
JO. Almost nine months.
JULES. Yes. This could have been one of the happiest days of our lives.
JO. I want to break your other leg so bad right now.
JULES. I'm just saying if we had followed the plan —
JO. — stupid plan —
JULES. — Our first attempt could have been —
JO. — emerging sickly from my vagina —
JULES. — and bravely struggling against all odds —
JO. — AS WE SLOWLY SUFFER, WASTE, AND DECOMPOSE.
BARBARA. I've been doing this job for a long long time. You should have seen this when I first got here.
JULES. Why is your arm in the tank?
JO. You'll never get me pregnant.
JULES. You could get a skin thing if you —
JO. There's water leaking in.
JULES. Are you trying to get a skin thing?
JO. Oxygen is low.
JULES. Are you trying to get the fish to eat your arm?
JO. We've been out of food for twelve days!
JULES. That's the surprise!
JO. There is no hope!
JULES. We can eat my leg. *(Barbara and Jules on separate tracks.)*
BARBARA. Did you know that when this exhibit opened they didn't have a drum?
JULES. I can't really feel anything below the knee.
BARBARA. They didn't have a pamphlet.
JULES. They're my largest muscles.
BARBARA. They didn't have me do anything except pull levers …
JULES. I've never been a fan of my thighs.
BARBARA. Show the emergency exits.
JULES. *(Pulling bourbon bottle out of bag.)* But, look!
BARBARA. Look how much I've improved it!
JULES. I could drink a lot of this, and you could saw it off before it gets too rotty —

JO. STOP! BEING! OPTIMISTIC! *(Barbara sighs. Overlapping a bit.)*

JULES. Biology is optimism —

JO. — motherfucking biology —

JULES. — A rebellion against Chaos!

JO. — it's not even a real science —

JULES. Take that, entropy.

JO. — Chemistry, physics: That's reality —

JULES. Animals don't give up!

JO. — And their cold forces are against us —

JULES. Jules will not give up.

BARBARA. I never gave up.

JO. Dorothy did. *(Beat.)*

JULES. Pardon?

JO. Your sister ran into a hurricane.

JULES. We agreed family was off-limits.

JO. In Kenya, did your other sister fight the hyenas?

JULES. There were six of them.

JO. Your entire family knew when it was time to go. Why are you the only one who doesn't know when to give up? *(Barbara cuts them off.)*

BARBARA. They are giving this up.

They called me into a meeting just before this. They sat me down with serious expressions. Quiet steady voices. Eyes that look like they cared but they don't.

"The attendance is low." "The technology is inefficient."

"Recent debate among the community at large has led us to doubt whether this story is even … *[true]*!" *(When Barbara hears Jules she backs away.)*

JULES. You've never told me about your parents.

BARBARA. Doubts?

JULES. I bet you had bad ones.

BARBARA. How can you doubt facts?

JULES. What did they do to you to make you such a … such a —

JO. My parents are dead. *(Beat.)*

JULES. Oh. I'm sorry.

How long ago?

JO. Not long.

JULES. Oh. *(Beat.)* How did they pass away? *(Beat.)*

JO. A FUCKING COMET HIT THEIR PLANET!

JULES. Right.
JO. Give up. Come on. You've failed. *(Jules looks around the lab, the sorry state, the door, the bag. Barbara sneaks out in front of the action again.)*
BARBARA. "Where is all the poop?" That's what the doubters always ask. "They've been there a long time, how did they reckon with the poop?" Do we really have to know everything to believe? A big hole. A pipe. There are ways. Do we really have to know precisely how … *[the poop gets out of the room]*?

Maybe they'll listen to you. If everyone here could write a letter to the management, express your support, share how much you appreciate …
JULES. I'm sorry.
BARBARA. I'm sorry. *(Beat.)*
JO. Go on. *(Over the next series of lines Jules walks around the room and picks up numerous objects and lines them up before Jo: knives, a plastic bag, blunt objects, duct tape …)*
JULES. I'm sorry for sealing this space, stocking supplies and even stealing a sonogram machine from the medical school, but then putting the majority of our food in a single, unstable room. That's not good enough for a moment like this.
JO. No, it isn't.
JULES. I probably shouldn't even have been a biologist. I should have listened to that persistent feeling of inadequacy and dread every time I went to class. I should have stuck to dance.
JO. You're not a dancer.
JULES. People thought my solo movement tribute to *Ontogeny Recapitulates Phylogeny* was really new and different. And it was. It — *(Jules starts to cry.)*
JO. Don't cry.
JULES. This sucks.
JO. Stop fucking crying.
JULES. Like a lot.
JO. Do you need to dance it out?
JULES. I thought I was going to be special.
JO. Oh, here it comes.
JULES. I thought this would be the moment I meant to show when I said, "I'll show you!"

I thought, hey Jules, you're alive, you're the only member of your family that's surviving. Do something. Honor them. Don't let your life go without doing something big. You are here to do something very big.

And I didn't.

You're right, Jo. I have failed. I HAVE FAILED! *(Jules drops a final object.)*

JO. Amen.

BARBARA. So have I.

JULES. It was supposed to be a little tribute to the way things work. The power and beauty of randomness. "Get on that Craigslist and see what the winds of chance bring you." It was poetic. It was perfect.

It was really stupid.

JO. You should have had interviews.

JULES. I should have.

JO. You couldn't have found a worse person than me.

I am the mistake! Apologize for that.

JULES. You suck happiness from a room. Like a vacuum that never loses suction. You're mean. You're atmospherically unpleasant. And you're physically abusive.

JO. That's self-defense, you fag.

JULES. I reject your phobia. I don't think you care enough about anything to really be a bigot. You just like to say bad words.

What you do believe in? What do you love? Is there anything that lights your candle or are you just Lady Scoffington of Hate Manor! Hi, I'm Lady Scoffington and I turn gold to shit and in my spare time I chisel words onto precious little tablets and waxywane about all the scoffy faggy hatefulness!

Write write write write write write write run to door boom motherfucker motherfucker write write write write write write write.

JO. What's with the stuff?

JULES. For someone who says they want to die all the time, you're not very good at it. Running into a door? Clearly not effective.

Almost grabbing the car battery, almost drinking formaldehyde, throwing debris in the air but collapsing out of the way before you get hit by it. And seriously, putting your arm in a fish tank is a pathetic way to end your days.

JO. I don't have a lot of options.

BARBARA. Neither do I.

JULES. Here are some more, depending on your taste. I'm not sure if you prefer something metaphorical or quick and dirty. *(Beat.)*

JO. However you want to do it.

JULES. What?

JO. Saw me. Throw the duct tape at me. Whatever floats your bone. Just make sure it works.

JULES. These are for you.

JO. I can't kill myself.

BARBARA. I can't breathe.

JULES. I am not going to be your dirty little death-whore! All I will do is provide you with tools and not stop you.

JO. If I was able to pick up that plastic bag and pull it over my face, I would have done it two hundred sixty-seven days ago. Don't you get it? I can't hurt myself. My body won't let me. Before the bag touches my head I'll be on the floor.

BARBARA. I need some air. *(Barbara has turned away from the action, some distance away from her console.)*

JULES. I know what we're doing here might be pointless. This struggle to keep on going. But I can't stop.

But, if your desire is not to fight until the bitter end then PLEASE WILL YOU TAKE SOME RESPONSIBILITY FOR YOUR FEELINGS AND JUST KILL YOURSELF ALREADY! *(Jo grabs a plastic bag, almost pulls it over her head. She expects a collapse/lever but it doesn't happen. She raises and lowers the bag. Again, no collapse. MAYBE, she looks over at the console from the corner of her eye? There is some realization, much like a tiger might have when she realizes that the pen she's been trapped in all her life is escapable. She pulls the bag fully, slowly suffocates and falls, seemingly dead. Jules looks at Jo on the ground.)* Motherfucker. *(Barbara sees Jo lying on the ground.)*

BARBARA. Motherfucker! *(Barbara runs to her station.)* Oh no oh no. That is not supposed to *[happen]*! *(Barbara pulls Jo's lever up and down. It has no effect.)*

Shoot. *(She pulls it again. Nothing.)*

Shoot shoot shoot. *(She pulls it several times and it pops out of the wall. Barbara screams. She pulls a different lever or button, the show freezes, stage dims.)*

Oh no oh no. Oh boy oh boy oh *[boy]*! *(Barbara frantically starts adjusting knobs and levers. Maybe she pulls out the operating manual. A phone rings at the control station. She answers it.)*

This is Barbara.

Just fine. Well, yes. Yes, I'm trying to address that situation right now. If I just push the … Yes, I know, technically, that's against policy, but this is the only time that this has happened … but I can't imagine that the outcome would be affected, especially if I … Mmm-hmm. Mmm-hmm.

I know I signed that. I … I don't understand. I mean, you've never really cared before. Well, maybe you're inappropriate! But … No. NO! Please, this is the last … just this one last time please let me — *(Barbara holds the phone away from her ear. After a yell on the other side of the receiver has finished, she hangs up the phone.)*

On behalf of the institution and its *[fucking]* management, I apologize for the errors made in today's presentation. I regret to announce that due to this, my error, I have been asked to cease the operation of this exhibit. "Immediately."

They would like me to leave. "With some dignity." Quote.

They said that if I hadn't added my own passion, my finesse, my percussion, and just stuck to the *[script]* that maybe "none of this would have happened." *(Sitting somewhere on the lab.)* How about that?

So where the red signs are, that's where you can … *(Barbara almost gives the gesture for exit but can't quite bring herself to do it.)* I wish I had control. I really wish that. *(Tears are flowing. She begins to exit … But something, the fish in the tank, catches her eye. She walks to the tank, perhaps putting her face on the glass, over the water? A turn.)* Look at you. Look at you in there moving about, on the verge, making decisions. *(A beat.)* If the first archaic cells on Earth just did what they were supposed to do, being generally unimpressive for millions of years instead of having that one day, literally one day, where two of them did something different, and merged and became a whole new thing … If that didn't happen many many times … Well then the rest of life wouldn't have happened.

None of this had to happen. But it did. And it's beautiful.

And they can take me out of here on a hook, but goddammit you are seeing the ending of this, even if it is going to be *[a little messed up]*.

So, remain seated, get comfy, watch how life unfolds and then we are all going out drinking and doing a motherfuckload of inappropriate things! *(Barbara does some frenzied version of a forced restart. A lever. Lights up. Jo is lying on the ground, bag on head. Elaborate frenzied movement and mutterings by Barbara. Her work requires quickness, perhaps having to perform some sort of acrobatic maneuver to hit two things at the same time. A switch springs Jules into action. He runs around back and forth in a panic.)*

JULES. Shoot shoot shoot. Please please please — *(Jules gets on top of Jo and begins CPR. Barbara kicks the side of the control panel or does some sort of hotwiring miraculous technical feat, Jo pops up and punches Jules in the face.)*
JO. HELLOOOO!
JULES. Ow.
BARBARA. Motherfucker!
JO. I'm alive.
JULES. *(Holding face.)* Yay.
BARBARA. Oh boy.
JO. I felt my lungs trying to pull in air but I couldn't.
JULES. There was a bag on your head.
JO. I felt the spinning, my knees buckling, I saw the colored spots.
JULES. You were losing oxygen.
BARBARA. My bad.
JO. I saw my entire life. Pages and pages of journals and diaries and I just reread them all.

I think I almost died.

JULES. That's why they say they're not toys.

I didn't think you'd actually do it.

JO. I never thought I could.
BARBARA. She couldn't.
JO. When I was born, I came out of the vagina and passed out. The doctors thought I had fluid in my lungs but, really, I was overwhelmed.
JULES. By birth?
JO. Its consequences. *(Barbara dums the timpani.)*

Every time danger lurks near me, it's a pressure in my head, as though the atmosphere is trying to crush my skull. If there's an oncoming car with a driver checking email on their phone as I enter a crosswalk, blam, I pass out safely on the curb. My parents used to hire me out to determine whether condemned buildings were safe to enter or if mine shafts were poisonous. I became known as "The Human Canary." Mysterious pseudo-death is an easy way to lose friends and spend a lot of time safe and alone, wondering why I'm worth so much protection.

JULES. You sense impending doom?
JO. It was getting so bad before coming here.
JULES. That's fantastic.
JO. The possibility of everything exploding …

JULES. Like an invisible shadow.
JO. Looms and renders me unconscious.
JULES. Just like a fish.
BARBARA. Of course, it's also a lever I'm pulling that renders her unconscious.

It has been a day!

JULES. You have a mechanism, some feedback loop of self-preservation that keeps you out of harm's way. No matter how hard you try. It's a brilliant —
JO. Mutation?
JULES. You have an amazing body! *(Beat.)*
JO. Thank you.
JULES. In the hospital my mother, dented and stained red by bricks, leaned forward right before she died, grabbed my hand and said, "My darling boy. Look at us. Look at your family and remember: Wherever you are, whatever you do, don't trust your instincts."

I think it's why I've never had sex.

JO. I haven't either.
JULES. Really?
JO. No.
JULES. Why haven't you?
JO. Something always went amiss.

I think it would help. Some contact to make me forget this fucking cosmic migraine whatever. Even a kiss would've been … One nice kiss. *(Beat.)*

JULES. I totally didn't think you were a virgin.
JO. What's that supposed to mean?
JULES. You were so forceful. Like you knew what you were doing.
JO. I practiced on a mannequin. *(Beat.)*
JULES. What kind of mannequin?
JO. Red Cross.
JULES. Ew! Fun. Ew.
BARBARA. I wish I had a mannequin. *(Beat.)*
JO. I don't want to die.
JULES. OK.
JO. I don't want to die.
JULES. I don't really want to either.
JO. But we're waiting.
JULES. We're alive.

JO. Do you really think there's a difference between what will happen in here and out there? *(Jo stares at Jules. Beat. Rising.)*
JULES. No.
JO. C'mon.
JULES. We can't.
JO. This is a trap.
BARBARA. It is.
JULES. Is that what your body is telling you?
JO. It doesn't need to.
BARBARA. Maybe there's a way.
JULES. We just need a new plan.
JO. Fuck plans.
JULES. There's got to be a way —
JO. A way out.
BARBARA. A way to find something better?
JULES. I don't want this to end.
JO. Everything ends.
JULES. I don't want to be alone.
JO. I WANT TO LIVE FOR THE LAST FEW MOMENTS OF OUR — *(Jules kisses Jo abruptly, probably not very romantically, but it's a kiss.)*
BARBARA. Oh my … That has …

That is the first time that has ever *[happened]*!

Oh I like this. (*Barbara pulls a lever, Jo and Jules freeze in the kiss.)* Oh, let's just linger in this moment. Before reality rushes in and drowns us. Let's linger and look at that and remain and relax and enjoy this.

I could open my own museum. *(Barbara pulls the lever. Jo pushes Jules away. This is quick.)*

JO. Hey hey hey!
JULES. Sorry.
JO. Jesus.
JULES. Sorry.
JO. God.
BARBARA. My own exhibit.
JULES. Sorry.
JO. Really.
BARBARA. I tell the story.
JULES. I just —
JO. No.

JULES. Sorry.
BARBARA. It would be much nicer when I make it. *(Barbara hits the timpani again very intensely. Jo flies onto Jules in another kiss. For both of then, this is kissing and contact of desperate, urgent need to fill a void of lifelong loneliness. They run into walls while they kiss, fall down, roll around maybe. But it's just kissing. Barbara is surprised and delighted by this. Perhaps she underscores. They stop kissing. They separate, panting, out of breath.)*
JULES. Was it bad again?
JO and BARBARA. No!
JO. That was better.
JULES. I wasn't sure about how much tongue —
JO and BARBARA. The tongue was fine.
JULES. OK. *(Beat.)* What about second base?
JO. No.
JULES. You sure?
JO and BARBARA. It would feel contrived. *(Barbara hits the timpani. Jo looks at the tank.)*
JO. Huh.
JULES. What?
JO. Is that JonJohn?
JULES. Swimming around Dorothy.
JO. That's really fast.
JULES. Bobbing up and down very impressively.
JO. They're crunking.
JULES and BARBARA. That's courtship!
JO. Yeah right.
JULES. It's what a male does to prove his strength to the female. He wants her to lay eggs in his part of the rock.
JO. This better not be an allegory.
JULES. It's rare for them to do that in a tank. *(Beat.)* OK.
JO. OK?
JULES. Maybe it's time, to, you know …
JO. Yes?
JULES. … See what nature has in store.
JO. It's our best shot.
JULES. I could have overlooked something
JO. It's beyond our control.
BARBARA. Would you come to a museum I opened?
JO. They look so happy.

JULES. I'm so glad and strangely amazed that neither of us decided to eat them. *(To the fish.)* You're on your own now.
JO. *(Writing.)* No matter the threat.
JULES. We've done what we can for you.
JO. No matter the odds.
JULES. Eat the algae when it grows.
JO. No matter the chaos that swirls.
JULES. You might have to eat one or two of each other. That won't be pleasant.
JO. Four little fish decide to look forward.
JULES. You could survive this with a little luck.
JO. In some small stupid way, that's sort of uplifting.
JULES. Make me proud.
JO. Don't forget us. *(Barbara laughs at the silliness of the idea of forgetting them.)* Ready?
JULES. Let's see what happens. *(Jo tosses the last notebook down. Jules walks to the door, opens it. It is a physically intense experience for him. He walks back to Jo. At some point they start to move with increasing speed towards the door as Barbara adds an increasing rumble on the timpani.)*
JULES and BARBARA. We could make it.
JO and BARBARA. We can.
JULES and BARBARA. This is good.
JO and BARBARA. There will be Sunlight.
JULES and BARBARA. And Happiness.
JO and BARBARA. And Joy!
JULES and BARBARA. And Bicycles!
JO and BARBARA. Flamenco Dancing!
JULES and BARBARA. Warmth!
JO and BARBARA. Fun Times!
JULES and BARBARA. Gentle Wind!
JO and BARBARA. Please.
JULES and BARBARA. Please.
JO and BARBARA. PLEASE —
JULES and BARBARA. PLEASE — *(Barbara's timpani rumbling rises to a crescendo as Jo and Jules run out the door. The timpani portion should have ended, but Barbara keeps hitting final booms on it. She doesn't want to stop. She finally throws the mallets like a rock star at the end of a concert. The tank bubbles.)*
BARBARA. I wrote that last part. Everything after she tosses the *[notebook]*.

What happens to them, specifically, after that is … *[unknown]*.

We can assume that it was quick. That the water outside rushed in swiftly, filling the room in a relative instant, reincorporating land back into the sea. *(She holds up a heavily deteriorated or somehow fossilized steno pad.)* The record only goes so far and all we know is that organisms of their line no longer *[exist]*.

I wish they knew what they did. That through their petty and adorable fun times they also saved our ancestors … *(Looking into the tank.)* … our four amazing ancestors who toughed it out in their little room, who reproduced, who survived. I wish we knew more about that part … those must have been a very difficult and amazing sixty-five million years.

Well, that's it. For now. Stay tuned, "Barbara's Museum of Epic and Intimate Events" will soon be under construction.

I love this story so much. I hope that you found it as *[fascinating]* as I do. And many people don't. Obviously.

I do get letters. From children. *(She pulls out a note.)*

"Dear Barbara,

Where do I come from? My mom and dad don't seem to know. Signed, Penny. Age eight."

Penny is adorable. And questioning. She deserves to know her history. We all do.

Penny: You come from Space. You come from millions and millions of lucky coincidences, sudden innovations, and steady pressure from an ever-changing landscape.

You come from ancestors that looked nothing like you … and from parents who sort of do. I don't know why there are people out there who don't want you to know how you came to be.

And what a beautiful Penny they've made. Beauty on the inside, but beauty nonetheless. *(Lighting focuses on the fish tank.)* And isn't it a lovely thing? That even when a large snow- and dustball flies in from space and obliterates nearly everything, there will always be a few.

And no matter what: The world will just keep on spinning and moving and changing and adapting and everything that we are, our substance, will always always … *(A gesture of eternity. Barbara walks back to her control center. She pulls a lever. All lights go out except for the tank. She pulls another lever and the tank lights go out.)*

End of Play

PROPERTY LIST

Fish food
Timpani, mallets
Backpack with steno pad, pen
Plastic cups, bottle of bourbon, ice
Plate of spanakopita
Charts, visual aids
Printouts, map
Tampons and diapers
Keys
Flashlight
Lanterns, candles
Cell phone
Plastic bag
Gong
Paper bag
Piece of paper
Knives, plastic bag, duct tape
Fossilized steno pad
Note

SOUND EFFECTS

Underscoring music
Sound of comet hitting the Earth
Phone rings

NEW PLAYS

★ **AGES OF THE MOON by Sam Shepard.** Byron and Ames are old friends, reunited by mutual desperation. Over bourbon on ice, they sit, reflect and bicker until fifty years of love, friendship and rivalry are put to the test at the barrel of a gun. "A poignant and honest continuation of themes that have always been present in the work of one of this country's most important dramatists, here reconsidered in the light and shadow of time passed." –NY Times. "Finely wrought…as enjoyable and enlightening as a night spent stargazing." –Talkin' Broadway. [2M] ISBN: 978-0-8222-2462-4

★ **ALL THE WAY by Robert Schenkkan. Winner of the 2014 Tony Award for Best Play.** November, 1963. An assassin's bullet catapults Lyndon Baines Johnson into the presidency. A Shakespearean figure of towering ambition and appetite, this charismatic, conflicted Texan hurls himself into the passage of the Civil Rights Act—a tinderbox issue emblematic of a divided America—even as he campaigns for re-election in his own right, and the recognition he so desperately wants. In Pulitzer Prize and Tony Award–winning Robert Schenkkan's vivid dramatization of LBJ's first year in office, means versus ends plays out on the precipice of modern America. ALL THE WAY is a searing, enthralling exploration of the morality of power. It's not personal, it's just politics. "…action-packed, thoroughly gripping… jaw-dropping political drama." –Variety. "A theatrical coup…nonstop action. The suspense of a first-class thriller." –NY1. [17M, 3W] ISBN: 978-0-8222-3181-3

★ **CHOIR BOY by Tarell Alvin McCraney.** The Charles R. Drew Prep School for Boys is dedicated to the creation of strong, ethical black men. Pharus wants nothing more than to take his rightful place as leader of the school's legendary gospel choir. Can he find his way inside the hallowed halls of this institution if he sings in his own key? "[An] affecting and honest portrait…of a gay youth tentatively beginning to find the courage to let the truth about himself become known." –NY Times. "In his stirring and stylishly told drama, Tarell Alvin McCraney cannily explores race and sexuality and the graces and gravity of history." –NY Daily News. [7M] ISBN: 978-0-8222-3116-5

★ **THE ELECTRIC BABY by Stefanie Zadravec.** When Helen causes a car accident that kills a young man, a group of fractured souls cross paths and connect around a mysterious dying baby who glows like the moon. Folk tales and folklore weave throughout this magical story of sad endings, strange beginnings and the unlikely people that get you from one place to the next. "The imperceptible magic that pervades human existence and the power of myth to assuage sorrow are invoked by the playwright as she entwines the lives of strangers in THE ELECTRIC BABY, a touching drama." –NY Times. "As dazzling as the dialogue is dreamful." –Pittsburgh City Paper. [3M, 3W] ISBN: 978-0-8222-3011-3